THE MP, AUNTY MANDY & ME

by Rob Ward

A BITTERSWEET TALE OF POLITICAL CAMPAIGNS, SEXUAL CONSENT AND STEAM TRAINS

Published by Playdead Press 2022

© Rob Ward 2022

Rob Ward has asserted his rights under the Copyright, Design and Patents Act, 1988, to be identified as the author of this work.

A CIP catalogue record for this book is available from the British Library.

ISBN 978-1-915533-08-1

Caution

All rights whatsoever in this play are strictly reserved and application for performance should be sought through the author before rehearsals begin. No performance may be given unless a license has been obtained.

This book is sold subject to the condition that it shall not by way of trade or otherwise, be lent, resold, hired out, or otherwise circulated without the publisher's prior consent in any form of binding or cover other than that in which it is published and without a similar condition including this condition being imposed on the subsequent purchaser.

Playdead Press
www.playdeadpress.com

The MP, Aunty Mandy & Me was first performed at Curve in Leicester on 3rd March 2020. It was an Emmerson & Ward Production in association with Curve. The company was as follows:

DOM	**Rob Ward**
Director	**Clive Judd**
Writer	**Rob Ward**
Producer	**Max Emmerson**
Dramaturg	**Beth Shouler**
Lighting Design	**Will Monks**
Sound Design	**Iain Armstrong**
Stage Manager	**Mason Cooper**

The production was revised for a 2022 tour, launching on 3rd August at Pleasance Dome as part of the Edinburgh Fringe Festival. It was an Emmerson & Ward Production in association with Curve. The company was as follows:

DOM	**Rob Ward**
Director	**Clive Judd**
Writer	**Rob Ward**
Producer	**Max Emmerson**
Assistant Producer	**Tabitha Rose Hughes**
Dramaturg	**Beth Shouler**
Lighting Design	**Will Monks**
Relighter	**Mischa Mah**
Sound Design	**Iain Armstrong**
Stage Manager	**Joe Colgan**

Rob Ward | Writer and Performer
Rob Ward is a writer, performer and co-director of Emmerson & Ward Productions. His 2013 play *Away From Home* (co-written with Martin Jameson) toured nationally and internationally between 2013 and 2015, picking up the Manchester Theatre Awards for Best New Play and Best Fringe Performance. His 2016 play *Gypsy Queen* has also toured nationally and internationally since it premiered on the West End (Arts Theatre) and has gained critical acclaim. In 2017 Rob was named one of the British Council's Emerging Artists. Both of these plays dealt with the subject of homophobia and LGBT+ visibility in sport as well as other takes on modern queer identity. Rob has since written *Conversations* (Digital production commissioned by Curve in 2021) and *Love It If We Beat Them* (commissioned by Live Theatre) is currently in development.

Clive Judd | Director
Clive Judd is a Director and Writer from the West Midlands. He trained on the National Theatre Director's Course; at the Watermill Theatre on the Regional Theatre Young Director Scheme; and was a member of the inaugural Foundry programme at the Birmingham Rep. Clive's play *Here* won the 2022 Papatango New Writing Prize. Directing credits include: *Macbeth* (Teatru Manoel, Malta); *Rails* (Theatre by the Lake); *Dyl, Sparks* (Old Red Lion Theatre); *This Will End Badly, Little Malcolm and His Struggle Against the Eunuchs* (Southwark Playhouse); *Captain Amazing, Rendezvous* (Live Theatre).

Beth Shouler | Dramaturg
Beth is a director, dramaturg and producer from the East Midlands with a passion for developing new work. She is

currently a Duffield Fellow 2022 on the Clore Leadership Programme and an emerging commercial producer on Stage One Bridge The Gap programme. Previously she was the New Work Associate and then Head of Creative Programmes at Curve, Artist Development Producer for Nottingham Playhouse, Young Company Director for Kiln and Lakeside Arts Centre, and Staff Director at Theatre Royal Plymouth. She was the first recipient of the In Good Company Mid-Career Commission to direct *I Dare You*. She co-founded Plymouth Fringe Festival, The Party Somewhere Else Collective and various festivals and artist development programmes.

Will Monks | Lighting Design
Will is a Leicester based Lighting and Video Designer; he trained at Bristol Old Vic Theatre School. Recent theatre work includes: *Petula* (National Theatre Wales), *Foxes* (Theatre 503, Seven Dials Playhouse; nominated for Best Lighting Designer: Offie Award), *Open Mic* (English Touring Theatre/Soho Theatre), *I Stand For What I Stand On* (National Tour), *The Great Big Story Mix Up* (Digital), *Sunnymead Court* (The Actors Centre and Digital, nominated for 4 Offie Awards), *I, Cinna (the poet)* (Unicorn Theatre; Winner of Theatre for Young People 12+ OnComm Award), *The Glass Will Shatter* (Omnibus Theatre), *Ali & Dahlia* (Pleasance London; nominated for Best Video Designer: Offie Award), *Trojan Horse* (UK tour, Edinburgh; winner of Fringe First and Amnesty International Freedom of Expression Awards), *The Snow Queen, Pinocchio* (Old Rep Theatre), *The Dark Room* (Theatre503; nominated for Best Lighting Designer: Offie Award); *Who Cares* (winner of Sit-Up Award), *We Live By The Sea* (nominated for Best Ensemble and Best Production: Offie Awards), *This Is Where We Live*

(International tours); *The Benidorm Elvis Fiesta* (Benidorm Palace).

Mishca Mah | Relighter

Misha Mah is a Production Manager, currently based in London. Theatre credits include: *Zombiegate* (Ameena Hamid Productions, Theatre503), *A Gig For Ghosts* (45North, Soho Theatre), *CASTE-ING* (Nouveau Riche, Roundabout), *Hungry* (Paines Plough, Roundabout), *Kabul Goes Pop: Music Television Afghanistan* (Brixton House, Touring), *Til Death Do Us Part* (Darcy Dobson Productions, Theatre503).

Iain Armstrong | Sound Design

Iain is a Composer and Sound Designer based in Birmingham, UK. His work is presented internationally and spans music and sound design for theatre, dance and film, experimental electronic music, multi-channel sound installation, site-specific soundwalks, podcasts, phonography and live performance. Recent credits include: music composition for Humanhood's dance works *ZERO* (mac Birmingham, Sadler's Wells) and *Orbis* (Without Walls, DanceXchange) and the soundtrack to Anna Falcini's film *Chère Julie*; theatre sound design for *The Glad Game* by Phoebe Frances Brown (R&D); *Rocket Fuel* by Little Earthquake (Mac Birmingham).

Joe Colgan | Technical Stage Manager

Joe Colgan is a UK based Production/Technical Stage Manager. Previous work includes No 1 musical touring shows, television, radio and live broadcasts, stage management (in stadia) for UK No1 selling music artists and most recently Sound Mixing for the world premiere of Rock, Paper, Scissors by Chris Bush at Sheffield Crucible.

Max Emmerson | Producer
Max is Executive Producer for Emmerson & Ward and Producer for Leeds Playhouse. He has worked as Executive Producer for Box of Tricks Theatre, Project Producer for ThickSkin Theatre, Interim Producer at Oldham Coliseum, Assistant Producer for the Royal Exchange Theatre and Bill Kenwright Productions in London. Producing credits include: *The Last Quiz Night on Earth* by Alison Carr (UK Tour), *Walk This Play Audio Series* by ThickSkin Theatre (Digital), *Conversations* by Rob Ward (Digital), *Sappho* by Daneka Etchells (R&D), *Sex/Crime* by Alexis Gregory (Soho Theatre), *Riot Act* by Alexis Gregory (UK Tour), *Don't Bother* by Broccan Tyzack-Carlin (Edinburgh Fringe Festival, Brighton Fringe & Manchester Fringe), *No Miracles Here* by The Letter Room (UK Tour), *Gypsy Queen* by Rob Ward (UK & International Tour), *SparkPlug* by David Judge (UK Tour), *The People Are Singing* by Lizzie Nunnery (Royal Exchange Theatre), *Adam & Eve & Steve* by Chandler Warren (Edinburgh Fringe Festival), *Shout! The Mod Musical* (Liverpool Royal Court Theatre).

Tabitha Rose Hughes | Assistant Producer
Tabitha is Assistant Producer for both Emmerson & Ward and The Octagon Theatre in Bolton. She is a recent graduate of the Management of Music, Entertainment, Theatre & Events degree at the Liverpool Institute for Performing Arts, and is the recipient of the 2022 Anthony Field Producer Prize and the Rising Star of the Year Award at the Queer Student Awards. Assistant Producing credits include: *The Last Quiz Night on Earth* by Alison Carr (UK Tour), *Love It If We Beat Them* (R&D), *The Book Thief* (Octagon Theatre, Bolton).

CHARACTERS

Dom Late 20s. Wannabe social media influencer and steam train enthusiast who lives in the small fictional town of Brinton in the north of England.

Mel Dom's scouse mum. Mid 50s.

Peter Local Labour MP who becomes Dom's boss. Late 40s.

Joey Dom's romantic interest. Mid 20s.

Alan Dom's quiz teammate and local Conservative candidate. Late 50s.

Graham Dom's Grindr hookup. Late 30s.

Ryan Dom's Instagram idol. Mid 20s.

Brintonian A disgruntled woman from Brinton. Early 60s.

Dom acts as the narrator of the piece through direct address. When he speaks to other characters his lines appear in "speech marks".

When **Dom** speaks as other characters this is indicated with the name of that character in brackets and the line in "speech marks".

All the action takes place in the small fictional northern town of Brinton.

One

DOM: The fastest steam locomotive in the world – ever – was the Mallard. Which is strange, because its named after a duck.

Three-cylinder design, double chimney and blastpipe. All designed by the genius that is Sir Nigel Gresley.

It wasn't just functional. It was beautiful. A big beautiful duck. In 1938 the Mallard hits its top speed of 126mph on a downward slope at Stoke Bank near Grantham.

The people in this country went mad for it cos the previous record was held by the Nazis.

And on 14th September of that year, it passes right through this very station. Through our little town. Brinton. Where nothing ever happens. Well that happened and that was history. History rattling along those tracks.

But this station is going. Reckon it won't last a year. No use for it anymore. No one leaves here and absolutely no one comes here. It'll just be old tracks and old tales. Then it'll be gone. And no one will never know the Mallard came here once.

I tell Graham this, thinking he'll be so turned on by the size of my brain that we'll fuck right here on the platform.

But he looks dead serious. Like that mountain in America with the faces.

(Graham) "It's only a fucking train."

"No. It's THE fucking train."

(Graham) "There's them trains in Japan what can go over two hundred."

Well this isn't going well.

I've been chatting to Graham for a few weeks now but this is our first meet. Date. Meet.

He was the nearest half decent gay I could find. Ten miles away.

I like him. He's got an edge. And he's chunky. Now ok, that's not a proper gay like in the pornos, but I'm partial to a chunky.

(Graham) "I best be off then."

"I thought we were gonna bum."

(Graham) "It's not called bumming. It's just shagging."

My chest tightens.

"Why don't we go for a drink?"

(Graham) "I don't want to."

"Please."

Breathing quicker now. Heart pounding.

He fucks off.

It's happening again.

Deep breath.

Deep breath.

Quicker.

And I'm shaking.

And quicker.

And I'm shaking still.

Two

DOM: I'm Dom. My name, that is. I'm actually a total sub bottom. But my name is Dom.

I am a hashtag instagay, hashtag influencer.

I'm just waiting for my first hundred like post. I did get ninety-seven for a gym selfie last week so we're getting there. I think the problem is I don't own a French Bulldog.

I wish I could be like Ryan. He's the King of the Instagays. Every post, three thousand likes minimum. Even when they're shit. Look at this one, it's just a photo of him with this top off, holding a pineapple, and it says "feeling prickly". I mean that's just shit.

Ryan has an onlyfans. I'm thinking of getting one too. Basically, it's a website were horny old gays pay you to stick things up your chuff.

All the power gays have onlyfans. Not that there's many power gays round here. There was a really hot guy who worked at the butchers. I tossed him off once behind the counter. But it didn't go anywhere. Well, it went on the chops but he just fed them to the dog.

He moved to the city eventually. All the gays move to the city. I can't go the city. Not with, y'know….

Dom mimics his anxiety attack from the first scene.

> I live with my mum. She likes to be called Melanie. I call her Mel.
>
> She's proper glam. Always "done up to the nines".
>
> I don't get that expression but my mum is always saying it about the neighbor she hates.
>
> My dad walked out on us years ago. Turns out he had another woman in the city. And another son. He lives with them now.

Simply Red's 'Fairground' to underscore the scene

(Mel) "Here he is, here's my handsome boy."

> Mum always calls me handsome which is nice, but it's hardly a thousand likes on insta is it?
>
> I read online a lot of divorced women turn to booze. My mum does bombs of MDMA. She calls them her Aunty Mandy.

(Mel) "Come and sit over here next to me and your Aunty Mandy."

"OK mum."

(Mel) "Mick Hucknall. Brilliant!"

"I know mum, you tell me that every time you play him."

(Mel) "I love the bones of you don't I?"

"You do."

(Mel) "And you love the bones of me don't you?"

"I do mum, yes."

(Mel) "And I don't care if you're gay as long as you're happy."

She's one of those older mums who has to remind you of that.

(Mel) "There's a lad who works at The Asda I think'd be good for you."

Mum's always trying to set me up with straight guys.

(Mel) "Lovely looking lad. Definitely gay."

"Has he said that?"

(Mel) "No. But I can tell."

"No mum, you can't tell."

(Mel) "Trust me, I can tell."

"You can't say that mum, it's a hate crime."

(Mel) "Oh everything's a hate crime these days. Anyway, never mind setting you up with a new fella, we need to set you up with a new job. Not having you dossing around this place on someone else's money."

"Like you, y'mean."

(Mel) "Cheeky little bastard. Your father left me a shithole house in a shithole town while he spends half the year swanning around Marbella. Now clear off bugger looks. Mike's coming over to lift me bonnet."

Mike works in a garage. It's called Mike + The Mechanics. He's mum's bit on the side.

She's right about the job. I could do with the money. I've seen this new cock ring online. All the gays wear cock rings now. I read somewhere that because they take so many drugs their willies don't work. But mine does, so it'd be purely decorative.

Three

DOM: Tuesday is quiz night. I play on a team with Alan. He's an old friend of my dad's.

He drinks those hand pumped ales. Calorific! I stick to a gin and slim.

I get back from the bar and hand him his change.

(Alan) "How much did that come to?"

"Deduct that from a tenner."

(Alan) "It's getting as bad as the Nelson in here. And have you seen that specials board? Chickpea curry. Did we ask for chickpea curry?"

"I ate before I came out."

(Alan) "No, not *we* we. I mean the collective *we*. We of this pub, of this parish, of this town. Did *we* ask for chickpea curry?"

"It's for the vegans."

(Alan) "It's getting too much this now."

"Honestly Alan, you can be a right gammon sometimes."

(Alan) "What's a gammon, when it's at home?"

"You!"

Sometimes you just have to tell them.

The first round is always pot luck and I'm always shit. I did once get a question on Drag Race. But there are no Drag Race questions tonight.

Second round. Capital cities. Alan is an expert. He's pissing it until...

(Alan) *(calling out to the quiz master)* "Excuse me, its called North Macedonia now. In fact, it hasn't been called the Former Yugoslav Republic for quite a few years!"

Alan turns in and talks to the team.

(Alan) "We can work this out. Let's go through the old Yugoslavia. Obviously, Serbia is Belgrade. Croatia, Zagreb. It can't be Ljubljana because that's Slovenia...."

Ten minutes later.

"...and if you go through the Baltic States you've got Estonia which is Tallinn, Latvia which is Riga. Lithuania is definitely Vilnius. I ended up there once on a booze cruise."

We don't get the answer. We have to leave it blank. Alan hates firing a blank.

Twenty minutes later we find out the answer is Skopje.

(Alan) "Bastard!"

The answer papers are handed in and we wait for the results.

Alan does politics. Like professional politics. He's the main Tory round here. I don't really do politics. Tonight, however, I've got a question for him.

"What are you going to do about the train station?"

(Alan) "What can I do lad, Labour's in charge round here."

"I thought the Tories were in charge."

(Alan) "We are nationally. But this is a Labour seat. Labour council. This mess is on them. You should speak to Peter Edwards."

"Who's he?"

(Alan) "Smarmy twat. He's your MP."

"And I can just speak to him?"

(Alan) "The cornerstone of our democracy! He'll be in his surgery on Friday?"

"Why, is he ill?"

(Alan) "No, not that surgery… you can go and see him on Friday. He'll be in the church hall."

"I will."

(Alan)	"You should. Tell him you're exercising your democratic right."
	"I will."
	Whatever that means.
	The results are in… and we've won!!
(Alan)	"Get in there you little beauty!"
	Alan waves his fist at a table of women and then he's off doing a victory lap around the pub.

Four

DOM: I'm in the church hall. There's a police officer with a yellow smoker's 'tache and an old man sat near me sucking on a Fisherman's Friend.

I'm here to exercise my democratic right.

It's my turn.

I stand over him. Peter Edwards.

Peter smiles at Dom.

He's got very white teeth.

(Peter) "Hello. How can I help?"

"I'm here to exercise my democratic right."

(Peter) "Good for you... and how do you intend to do that?"

"By exercising it."

(Peter) "By exercising what?"

"My democratic right!"

Who voted for him? He's proper thick.

(Peter) "Look, why don't you start again and just tell me what the problem is?"

I let him have it. Both barrels. I tell him about the train station closing and how I'm not happy about it. I watched that TV show with my mum once, the one where everyone in the audience is angry and they shout at the politicians. They tell them it's a disgrace. I give it a go.

"It's a disgrace!"

(Peter) "Look, I appreciate and admire your passion on this subject, but let me assure you, as long as I am your MP I would rather chain myself to the tracks than lose that station. I'm going to raise it at Prime Minister's Questions."

I'm not sure what that is but it sounds filthy.

(Peter) "I will do everything in my power to save our station."

He's good. He's very good.

Peter smiles.

Smiles again. Pearly white. Almost too white.

(Peter) "So... are you a member of a party?"

"Influencers don't do politics."

(Peter) "Influencers?"

"We don't want to risk losing fans."

(Peter) "Oh."

"And my mum says you're all liars."

(Peter) "Does she now?"

Pause.

(Peter)   "So who are these fans of yours?"

"I don't know if you've heard of Instagram."

(Peter)   "Christ. You don't think I'm *that* old?"

"Sorry, I didn't mean…"

(Peter)   "I'm teasing. I can picture you on Instagram. Plenty of likes."

"Yeah."

(Peter)   "You work in marketing then?"

"No. Too cold in the winter."

(Peter)   "No… I don't mean market stalls… digital marketing. Social media?"

"Oh! I'd like to, I guess, but, not sure where to start."

Peter considers this.

(Peter)   "Maybe I can help."

"Oh?"

(Peter)   "My team are looking to offer someone a paid internship. Why don't you pop along to my office next Friday when I'm back from London?"

Wasn't expecting that. I sort of mumble something and he says…

(Peter)   "What?"

"Watt invented the steam train."

Peter looks bemused.

"James Watt. He invented the steam train. Well, technically you can't give him all of the credit but he's generally recognized as the key player."

(Peter) "You learn something new every day."

"I like trains. Steam trains."

(Peter) "Steam trains and social media. Well I won't keep you. What with it being a Friday I imagine you'll want to be getting home. Plans with the girlfriend this evening?"

"I don't have a girlfriend. I'm gay. A gay homosexual and I'm proud."

You have to say that otherwise the straights win.

(Peter) "Good for you. Well, she'd best move on. Captain Birdseye over there has a problem with his tractors. Make sure you swing by the office next Friday. Let's see what we can do."

He just called himself *she*.

Five

DOM: Next Friday comes around.

Mum's bought me a new suit from Matalan. If anyone asks its Paul Smith.

She's pleased for me. But she's not pleased who it's with.

(Mel) "Don't you come back here a Blairite bastard."

I meet his team and spend the morning getting up to speed on his twitter. I tell them we need to get him on Insta, TikTok and Snap. Everyone knows twitter is dead.

Peter takes me out for the afternoon. He's unveiling a statue in the town centre. Some local bloke who did something for farming once. They love that shit round here.

He wants me to film it.

(Peter) "Right Spielberg, you set up over here and try grab us the money shot."

Peter takes to the microphone.

(Peter) "Well good afternoon everyone. Good to see so many of you here."

There's about eight people.

(Peter) "Today we honour one of our finest Brintonians. Through his innovative work on the design of the modern-day manure spreader,

	Lord William Claude Moss really changed the game in the field of pest control and helped farmers, not just in Brinton, but across the whole of the UK."
	The microphone squeaks. A woman next to me grunts.
(Brintonian)	"Loves himself this fella."
(Peter)	"We're very lucky to be joined today by Alma Moss…"
	That's a silly name.
(Peter)	"Alma is the great granddaughter of Lord William."
	Suddenly, a group of grey men turn up.
(Alan)	"What about the train station Edwards? You had that meeting with the Prime Minister yet?"
	It's Alan!
(Alan)	"Promised us he'd save the station didn't he folks?"
(Peter)	"Thank you Alan…"
(Alan)	"So have you had that meeting?"
(Peter)	"Alan, I don't think…"

(Alan) "He's not answering the question folks! Can you believe that? A politician not answering the question."

(Brintonian) "You're all liars".

(Alan) "And what about our NHS folks? It's on its knees, isn't it?"

(Peter) "Thank you Alan, you've made your point. Today is a day of celebration."

(Alan) "Celebration!?! What's there to celebrate folks? Our NHS, your NHS, is on its knees. And anyone can use it these days, can't they?"

(Peter) "Alan this is neither the time nor the place..."

(Alan) "This is our NHS. It's your NHS."

(Brintonian) "It's my NHS!"

(Alan) "This country is changing. First its chickpea curry down the Crown and Anchor. And did you read the papers this morning? The BBC are insisting the tooth-fairy is gender neutral."

(Peter) "Alan this is ridiculous!"

(Alan) "There is an election coming folks. And that is your chance to give your verdict on your local MP, Peter Edwards!"

Six

DOM: We're back in the office.

(Peter) "I knew he'd do something like this! He's been waiting for the publicity. He is fighting a guerilla campaign. And where the fuck was security!?! Right, everyone outside for a moment I need some thinking time. Dom you stay. See if we can salvage something on twitter."

Dom isn't sure what to do. Peter has a moment to calm himself down.

(Peter) "Sorry you had to see that."

"I know Alan."

(Peter) "You do?"

"I'm on his quiz team."

(Peter) "If you're working in this office, you need a new quiz team."

"He was friends with my dad."

(Peter) "Your dad needs new friends."

"My dad fucked off years ago. Haven't seen him since."

Peter takes a moment.

(Peter) "Sorry."

"Alan was there for my mum. She doesn't like Tories but he's been good to her."

(Peter) "I can't get anything right today, can I?"

Peter studies Dom for a moment.

(Peter) "You're a very impressive young man."

"Am I?"

(Peter) "I've been watching you today. You're exactly what this office needs."

Does that mean?

(Peter) "The job is yours if you want it."

"Thank you. I don't know what to say."

(Peter) "Well luckily, I do."

He reaches into a cabinet and pulls out a bottle of wine and two glasses.

"Wine o'clock honey. She's in desperate need!"

He called himself *she* again.

"Peter can I ask you something? You called yourself she. Are you…"

(Peter) "Into musical theatre?"

"Yes."

(Peter) "Jackpot! Congratulations honey, you've won a trip to Disneyland."

"Me too."

(Peter) "I know, you told me. Besides, I could tell."

"How?"

Peter shoots Dom a look as if to say 'it's obvious'.

"I always thought I could pull of masc for masc."

(Peter) "Ha! Well honey it's nice to have a comrade in the trenches."

"Promise I won't tell anyone."

(Peter) "Oh tell away. I already have."

"I didn't know you could be a gay politician. I thought it was like being a vicar."

(Peter) "You have to be a good gay. The Guardian did a feature on me and my husband last year. Homemade jam. Nights at the theatre. Wholesome middle-class bummers who won't threaten the heteronormative status quo. To be a successful gay man in politics you can't have a cock."

He's so funny. Most gays think they're funny, but he actually is.

Then we talk about things I've never talked about. That no one round here talks about. That I don't know how to talk about.

(Peter) "We need a night out."

"Do we?"

(Peter) "Fancy it?"

Shit.

"I can't."

(Peter) "What? With an arse like yours you'll be a hit."

"I know, but I can't. I have this thing..."

I explain my problem and how it gets worse with lots of people around.

(Peter) "Oh you poor love. Well you know I'd look after you."

I reckon he would, y'know.

I'm not sure where this comes from, but I ask...

"Peter. Have you spoken to the Prime Minister about the station?"

Peter didn't expect this.

(Peter) "Well it's not quite as simple as that Dom. The conversation is moving in the right direction, though it has the tendency to take an occasional detour. Big boy politics I'm afraid. But we like a big boy. Let me know if you change your mind about that night out. We'd have a lot of fun."

Seven

(Mel)   "You have a good time love. You are handsome. I hope one of them gays can see that. And pick a goodun. Not a twat like your father."

Peter drives us over to his apartment. He tells me about his husband who works away a lot. He's quite mean about his husband, but he's gay, so that means he loves him.

His advice is

(Peter)   "Marry a man with money. Preferably one who's never home."

He has a hall pass tonight. He has one most nights, even if he doesn't ask for one.

His place is amazing. Obviously. There's a balcony with a view across the city, which is mainly just buildings and roads. But nice buildings. Nice roads.

And a hot tub. A fucking hot tub!

My eyes get drawn to this picture on the wall. Except it's not a picture its words.

"They fuck you up your mum and dad."

Peter is watching me as he's mixing the pornstar martinis.

(Peter)   "Philip Larkin. Have you read his work?"

"Oh yeah. All of it."

(Peter) "He was a violent man my dad. Ex-military. He wanted his son to be Marc Anthony, instead he got Cleopatra."

I don't know who either of those people are but it's so funny.

(Peter) "Let's be outrageous. Worst sex you've ever had?"

"This is mad."

(Peter) "Come on there must be a few grim tales in Brinton."

"You don't get anything in Brinton."

(Peter) "What! Not even a horror story set in a farmer's field?"

"I don't do it outdoors. My mum says I feel the cold."

(Peter) "Well, where's the most outrageous place you've ever had sex?"

"I stuck a finger up my bum in a church toilet when I was fifteen."

(Peter) "Oh honey we're going to have to bring you out of your shell, aren't we?"

I hope he does. I'd love to be more outrageous. Like in the pornos.

(Peter) "What underwear have you got on?"

"Dunno. My mum buys mine from Primarni."

(Peter) "Let's have a look."

Oh.

(Peter) "You need to have good underwear love. You don't want to let the gays down do you?"

He's right, I don't.

Dom pulls his jeans down to reveal his colorful (and awful) underwear.

(Peter) "SOS. We can't have you going out in those."

He goes out the door and into the next room.

I've never talked to another gay like this before. I mean, I've liked photos and sent flaming emojis, but never talked. It's nice.

He comes back in and hands me a really hot jock. He's excited. He says he has another surprise.

Peter reveals a dog mask.

(Peter) "This is how I don't get noticed. It's leather and fetish night at Purge. You're going to love it."

"Do you do this all the time?"

(Peter) "Well as the good married gay MP I can hardly swan into the local cruising bar and ask Polly to put the kettle on. If you're worried about other people looking at you then just do what I do. Put on the mask."

So I do.

Dom puts on the dog mask. We are transported through a cacophony of sound and light into the nightclub Purge.

There are so many different types of gays in here.

Muscly ones and sexy ones, fat ones and thin ones, hairy ones and scary ones.

And they're dancing.

And I'm dancing.

It's sweaty. It's sexy.

(as Peter) "See him over there…"

Peter points at some twink who is bouncing between two bears.

(as Peter) "John Coley. Holy Coley they call him. He can sit on a traffic cone."

On a traffic cone? Wow. He's a gay icon.

I go for a piss and there's guys checking me out at the urinals.

One of them is looking at my cock.

One of them squeezes my arse.

And one of them drags me into a cubicle.

I come out and I tell Peter. He's loving it.

And the next thing, he's down on all fours and he's drinking a gin and slim out of a dog bowl.

Suddenly at the bar, I see him. Ryan. King of the Instagays.

I look at Peter.

Peter gestures with his head for Dom to go for it.

Fuck it.

I walk over to him.

He's stood looking out. He's a giant.

"Excuse me, its Ryan isn't it?"

(Ryan) "Yeah."

"I'm an influencer like you and I have so much respect for you. I need to know, how do you get more likes?"

(Ryan) "I never smile."

"Never?"

(Ryan) "Never. No filter for laughter lines babes."

Of course. So I stop smiling and I walk around the club like a bad ass.

We get back to the apartment. The sofa eats me up.

He sticks some music on. I have to sort the tunes out. No one's listening to Chilled Ibiza anymore.

He hands me a capsule. I recognise this.

"My mum calls this her Aunty Mandy."

I tell him about my mum. He finds it hilarious.

I guess it is.

He takes one.

I think about my mum.

What she'd think.

And I take one.

And another.

And the hug from the sofa gets deeper and warmer.

(Peter) "Can I say something?"

"Yeah."

(Peter) "This makes me very happy."

"Me too."

He comes over and gives me a hug. The sofa is hugging me and Peter is too.

(Peter) "You've very quickly become one of my favourite people."

"You too. You're the best gay I know."

(Peter) "Well honey there isn't much competition."

They laugh.

(Peter) "I think as really good friends we should have another Aunty Mandy, a pornstar martini and a hot tub."

"Oh my god yes."

And now I'm getting a hug in water.

(Peter) "I love you, you know."

"No..."

(Peter) "You're clever and funny and most importantly sexy."

"You reckon?"

Peter places his hand on Dom's leg.

(Peter) "I'm going to bed. I think you should join me."

And I stop.

I think.

He's been so good to me.

The job.

Tonight.

This.

I owe him.

I say yes.

The only thing I can say.

He touches me.

I don't go hard.

I try really hard.

I can't let him down.

I go hard.

And he sucks.

He sucks.

He sucks so hard he nearly sucks it off.

He kisses me.

He tastes of fags.

He licks my arse.

His chin is grizzly.

But I moan.

For him.

It's what friends do.

He says he has a special trick.

He takes my hand.

Makes it a fist.

And he sits on it.

And he bounces.

And he bounces.

And he bounces.

And he jizzes all over me.

He falls asleep.

Head on my chest.

The MP, Aunty Mandy and Me.

Eight

DOM: The drive back is quiet. I pretend to be asleep. He drops me off near the old mill.

(Peter) "Bright and early tomorrow morning."

"Can't promise."

(Peter) "Thanks love. To know I have a friend like you and we can have adventures like that... it means a lot to me."

"No one has ever said I mean a lot to them."

(Peter) "Well they should. You're a goodun. Now go on, bugger off."

He drives away.

A blast of 'Stars' by Simply Red

(Mel) "Oh here he is the dirty stop out."

Two o'clock on a Sunday afternoon and mum is drowning in Aunty Mandy.

"Sorry mum."

(Mel) "Jesus the state of you. Are you on something?"

"No."

(Mel) "Are you sure?"

"Mum, you're on something every day."

(Mel) "That's different. I've had hardships. You've had fuck all."

"I'm not on anything I'm just hungover."

(Mel) "Who is this mysterious friend of yours?"

"No one."

(Mel) "Is it a *special* friend?"

"Mum!"

(Mel) "Oh ey, check out Casanova *(singing badly)* It must be love, love, love, du-duh."

Nine

DOM: A few months go by. Things are going really well. I'm getting a hundred-plus likes every post. It's all about the hashtags hun.

There's an election coming.

I'm knocking on doors for Peter. Some people like him, some people really don't. One man got very angry about the bins not being taken out. He said it's a load of rubbish.

I don't go the quiz as much. It wouldn't be fair to Peter, what with Alan being the main Tory. Besides, the one time I did go, he was just kicking off on the quizmaster.

(Alan) "Sue Barker never won Wimbledon you dozy pillock!"

I saw him out on the campaign trail once. He smiled at me. I didn't smile back. He's such a gammon.

I've got money too. Proper money. Which is great because I can move out soon. My mum is doing my head in. Today is my birthday. But when I came downstairs this morning she was just passed out on the sofa.

They've put up a banner for me in the office. Joan from finance has baked a cake, which looks shit, but I was brought up better than to say that.

"Thanks Joan."

Dom spots someone.

Oh. Who's he?

He's fit.

Happy Birthday Me.

"Honey!"

Peter calls me into the office.

(Peter) "Let's leave the squares out there!"

Peter has a present for Dom. An enormous dildo.

(Peter) "Happy birthday love!"

"Thanks. Who's the new lad?"

(Peter) "He's joined us for the campaign from a CLP in Cheshire. And honey, do I have some birthday gossip for you."

Gossip to gays is like spinach to Popeye.

(Peter) "She's on our team."

"Labour?"

(Peter) "No you doughnut. She's one of us."

"No!"

(Peter) "Well, under the same umbrella. Bisexual."

Wow. Just when the people of Brinton had got used to gays.

"What did you say he's going to do?"

(Peter) "Bend over and take it like a goodun! Relax. You know me, consummate professional. Get this, his name is Joey."

Silly name. Only kangaroos are called Joey.

(Peter) "Came in this morning. Proper little chatterbox. Was telling me all about the problems with his ex-girlfriend. Breeders. What are they like? Gorgeous eyes, hasn't he?"

Oh.

He reaches into his wallet and pulls out a couple of capsules.

"In work?"

(Peter) "Honey, I've had a hell of a morning. I need to take the edge off."

And after he takes the edge off, he takes the rest of the afternoon off. Drives me back to his and he gets me off.

Dom feels judged. He confronts the audience.

He is my best friend. It is my birthday.

Ten

In this scene, play around with sound and light and pauses between dialogue to create a trippy, drug-fueled ambience.

DOM: I float back home.

Simply Red's 'Holding Back The Years' underscores the scene.

          Mum is off her tits.

          She's lying on her back and conducting an invisible orchestra in the sky.

(Mel)   "Here he is! The handsome birthday boy. Mick Hucknall. Brilliant."

Dom doesn't respond.

(Mel)   "Where have you been?"

Dom doesn't respond.

(Mel)   "Oh you've been with that Blairite bastard. When's he gonna come and fix me drains?"

          "How much have you had?"

(Mel)   "Enough to take the edge off. Your tea's in the oven. Why's he got you working till this time on your birthday?"

          "We went for a drink."

(Mel)   "Present's on the table."

Dom picks up a model train.

The City of Truro. The Great Western Railway lot will tell you it was faster than the Flying Scotsman. The original Scotsman, not the commercial engine we know today.

(Mel) "That's the one you wanted isn't it?"

"Thanks mum."

I go into the kitchen to see what's for tea. Open the oven door. Whatever it was its burnt to fuck.

(Mel) "Oh no, no, no! I completely lost track of time."

"Why are you such a mess?"

(Mel) "You know what your Aunty Mandy can be like."

"She's fine for me."

(Mel) "Has that Blairite been feeding you drugs? I should go to the papers."

"No mum. Just fuck off will you, you old wreck head."

(Mel) "Get to your room!"

"As if! I'm going out mum."

(Mel) "You are not. It's your birthday and we are gonna spend it like a family."

"You can throw that present away."

Mum has a tear in her eye but I don't fall for it. I'm out the door, pounding the pavement, all the way to Peter's. He lets me in, and I cry a bit too.

He says I can stay tonight.

He's so kind.

As we're watching TV he slides his hand down.

Eleven

DOM: Joey is hot.

He's having a brew while he reads his phone.

"So what's it like being bisexual?"

(Joey) "Excuse me?"

"Sorry, that didn't come out right."

(Joey) "Ah well, neither did I."

"Neither did you?"

(Joey) "Come out right."

Dom gets it. He grins.

"Joey?"

(Joey) "Yes. Joey the Cheshire bisexual. And you are? Peter didn't say."

"I'm Dom."

Now he's got a different look. I like this look.

"Do you have insta-bis like we have instagays?"

(Joey) "What?"

"Watt invented the steam train."

(Joey) "Did he though?"

"What?"

(Joey)   "James Watt. Did he invent it or did he just advance the design of Thomas Savery?"

                       Wow.

                       "Savery's wasn't a commercial engine."

(Joey)   "Does that matter?"

                       I am so turned on.

                       "Are you into trains?"

Joey laughs.

(Joey)   "My dad was an engineer. Worked on them for years."

                       So, we chat a bit more train. He's got the cheekiest smile. And he's smart.

                       I can see Peter watching from his office.

                       "Have you been to the station yet?"

(Joey)   "No. Been meaning to check it out."

                       "I could show you. If you like?"

(Joey)   "Yeah?"

                       "Not much else to do round here."

(Joey)   "You're on then."

                       "What?"

Joey winks.

(Joey) "Watt invented the steam train."

Dom smiles. Peter appears.

(Peter) "She moves fast."

How long has he been there?

"He's into trains. You said gays don't like trains."

(Peter) "I'm delighted for you honey but I can't stop. Westminster is calling me like a siren onto the rocks."

But he stops and talks to Joey. Then he leaves.

Twelve

DOM: We're on a date. He's wearing a shirt.

We've gone to the station so he could check it out. He didn't want to sit so we're strolling up and down the platform.

It's weird, but I don't mind.

"The Prince of Penrith will be in Pipping later this year."

(Joey) "Oh right. Is that an A1?"

"A3. Come on."

(Joey) "Of course. Sorry mate, I'm not much company. Not sure where my head is at right now."

I go back to trains. I tell him the story of the Mallard. Tell him the station is closing. Peter's done fuck all so far.

(Joey) "How long have you worked for him?"

A flash of Peter.

"Since the start of the year."

(Joey) "He's so funny."

Another flash of Peter. Dom is disturbed.

"I think we should talk about you."

(Joey) "He doesn't give a shit does he?"

The strongest and most disturbing flash of Peter yet.

"He doesn't no. But I really think we should talk about you."

And suddenly it's like he's watching us.

Peter.

He's not too happy.

Shit.

My chest tightens.

Deep breath.

Not here. Not now.

(Joey) "Are you ok?"

"Yeah... I just have this thing..."

(Joey) "Oh shit, are you having a panic attack?"

"Great first date this."

(Joey) "I've had worse. Just breathe. You're ok. We can just stay here and chill."

Dom starts to calm down.

And everything slows down.

I'm good.

I tell him he's alright really.

(Joey) "Not sure my ex would agree."

	"Can I ask what happened?"
(Joey)	"We'd gone stale. We both knew it. Couldn't talk. So, I decided to do the mature thing. Went out, got shitfaced, fell asleep on the sofa whilst I was on Grindr… guess who came downstairs and saw."
	"No!"
(Joey)	"Yup. Safe to say that ended that one."

He looks genuinely sorry. I don't know where this comes from, but I put my arm around him.

We are staring at each other.

And we kiss.

I can't quite believe he's kissing me back.

(Joey)   "I'd like to do this again."

"Me too."

I think I have a second date.

Thirteen

(Peter)   "A train station hey?"

                     "How do you mean?"

(Peter)   "Joey told me all about your romantic choice for a first date."

                     "I think it went well."

(Peter)   "Just remember to be careful love. He's new on the scene. He'll want to have lots of filthy sex before he settles down again. Don't get too close."

                     "But I really do think it went well."

(Peter)   "A train station!"

For a moment, Dom snaps.

                     "A train station that you promised to save, Peter."

Peter turns.

(Peter)   "Oh! Listen to Martha Scargill. Leave the politics to the grownups, Dom. Now if you'll excuse me, I have to pack."

                     "You told me you could save it. Remember?"

(Peter)   "I have to pack."

Fourteen

DOM: At the end of the week, Peter takes some of us from the office out for a drink. We go to the city. Not to Leather and Fetish night, I'm not sure Joan from finance could handle that. We go to a posh bar instead.

Joey is with me. But a lot of his time is spent chatting with Peter.

I squeeze his arse.

(Joey) "Easy tiger."

(Peter) "Honey, save it for the bedroom. Or should I say the train station?"

He laughs. Joey sort of half laughs.

Peter goes for a piss.

"I am here you know."

(Joey) "I know mate. Pete is giving me some good advice. I don't wanna be rude."

I squeeze his arse again.

(Joey) "Could you not, Dom? I don't want to make Pete feel like a third wheel."

More drinks. By this point, everyone else has gone. It's just the three of us.

Joey goes the bog for an Aunty Mandy.

Peter leans in. Brings me close. Closest in weeks.

(Peter) "I saw him first, remember."

"What?"

(Peter) "I saw him first and I've done all the hard work. It isn't fair you swanning in and playing the knight in shining armour."

I step back and look at him. He turns away. Scans the room.

Joey comes back. They're best mates again.

I stare at Joey. And Peter.

And I see it now. I see what this is.

Dom is gripped by a bad panic attack.

Now I'm feeling something else.

This is gonna be a bad one. Really bad.

"Just going the bog."

I burst out the front of the pub and knock the bouncer.

I ask him for help. I'm shaking.

Call an ambulance!

Joey can't help this time. He'd probably make it worse.

Deep Breath.

Deep.

Breath.

Fifteen

DOM: I could have said no. He didn't force me. But I couldn't say no.

Why did you let him do it?

I can't really answer that question.

He made me feel good.

He said I was smart.

He said I was sexy.

That's very important.

But he's done with me.

"He wants you now Joey."

Joey stares for what feels like forever, then offers me a cold hug.

(Joey) "But you're ok now?"

"I'm telling you because I know he wants to do the same thing to you."

(Joey) "How do you know that?"

"I just know."

(Joey) "So are you and him…?"

"What?"

(Joey) "Finished?"

	"We weren't together."
(Joey)	"Oh... no... I mean..."
	"Have you not listened?"
(Joey)	"Sure."
	"Joey?"
(Joey)	"Look I know it's weird when you get with your mates. That's why I always avoided it."
	"Get with your mates?"
(Joey)	"...and its difficult because he's married and... I dunno."
	"What?"
(Joey)	"Invented the steam train."

Joey smiles. Nothing.

(Joey)	"I can believe it's difficult for you Dom, but I don't believe that's how it happened."
	"But it did."
(Joey)	"I believe that you believe it."
	"So why don't you?"
(Joey)	"Well it's just what happens with you guys isn't it?"
	"You guys?"
(Joey)	"You shag your mates."

"Oh."

(Joey) "Guys are horny aren't they? I know I am."

He turns to leave.

"Wait Joey. What about trains? Well it's not really about trains, but in a way it kind of is because… we're good aren't we? It kind of works. And that's great. Cos I didn't think I'd ever meet someone like you."

I can feel Peter breathing down my neck.

(Joey) "I don't feel comfortable with this Dom. I'm sorry."

Sixteen

DOM: I don't hear from Joey that night. Or the next morning. I ring in sick.

WhatsApp from Peter. Can I come over tonight? We need to talk.

My mum is away at the moment so I agree.

I know how I can make it up to him.

And he deserves that.

Because he's been good to me.

I know where my mum's secret stash of Aunty Mandy is.

I've taken one.

Two.

(Peter) "How are you Dom?"

"Been better."

(Peter) "Joey told me it didn't work out. I'm sorry love. I think he just wants time to be single for a while doesn't he? Have some fun."

Dom says nothing.

(Peter) "He also told me something interesting."

Peter's tone changes.

(Peter) "He's become a very good friend has Joey. He told me what you've been suggesting."

"I'm not suggesting though, am I Peter?"

(Peter) "I've been in politics for a while. It's a calling Dom. To help people. It's a real honour to do what I do. What you've said about me? I have to admit, I'm really worried about you."

"Don't be."

(Peter) "I really am. I don't know what's going on in your head but I don't think you're well at the moment. You're isolating yourself, you're forgetting who your friends are. You're better than this"

"I don't want to be lonely."

(Peter) "No love. None of us do. It all got complicated didn't it? You see, this is why the stable boys should never mix."

"I'm sorry."

(Peter) "I know."

He starts to undo his belt.

I drop to my knees.

And I make it up.

He cums.

He zips.

He leaves.

After a moment Dom slowly stands up and reveals his phone. He plays back the video he has just secretly captured of him and Peter.

Dom smirks.

Seventeen

DOM: He opens the door.

Deep breath in.

(Alan) "Let me guess, you've come to your senses and you're voting Tory?"

"Can I speak to you?"

Alan can tell I'm serious.

He leads me into the front room. Unsure of what to say.

(Alan) "Can I get you a tea, coffee… there's a few bottles of Bombardier in the fridge…"

"I'm good."

(Alan) "You don't look it."

"I've got something that I think will help you."

(Alan) "Oh?"

Dom takes the phone out and places it in front of him.

"I've had sex with a married man."

(Alan) "Right… well… I…"

"Peter Edwards."

I tell him it. All of it.

He doesn't say a thing for probably the longest period of time Alan has never said a thing.

Dom gestures to the phone.

"I want you to use it. Ruin him. Finish him."

Then the weirdest thing. Alan just puts an arm around me.

(Alan) "Oh lad. I don't know what to say. I am so sorry to hear this. This is awful Dom."

"Use it Alan. I want you to destroy him."

(Alan) "No Dom. I'm not doing that."

"But they'll slaughter him for this."

(Alan) "It's not that creep I'm worried about. I'll beat him at the ballot box. I'm more concerned about you."

"But I want you to do it."

(Alan) "I know how this goes lad. You'd be the one breaking up a marriage, you'd be the problem. And in this small town?

Beat.

(Alan) "Have you talked to your mam?"

"I can't. Not while she's away."

(Alan) "Aye. For the best. Fuck the Bombardier, I think we need the Single Malt."

Eighteen

> Election Night. I'm in the church hall. They're on the stage. There's Peter, Alan and one candidate dressed as Big Bird.
>
> Peter's trying to smile. Trying.
>
> A posh man addresses the crowd. It's the number of votes.
>
> Alan...

(Returning Officer) "23,788"

> Peter...

(Returning Officer) "24,251"

> People in red rosettes start cheering.
>
> 500 votes in it.
>
> Alan didn't do anything with the video.
>
> We did the right thing.

(Peter) "I promised the people of Brinton, a vote for me is a vote to prioritise local issues. A vote for me is a vote for a better Brinton. And a vote for me is a vote to save our local railway station. As promised, Monday morning I will be down in Westminster and I'll be demanding a parliamentary review into the planned closure of the station."

He's drowned out by applause. He loves applause.

But right now he's just staring out. Taking it in.

He catches my eye.

Eyebrow rises. Just a touch. Eyeballs widen. Just a tad.

He can see me. He knows I'm here. He knows I see him.

And then he's gone.

Nineteen

DOM: A month later.

It's the Annual Railway Gala. There's bunting and cake sales and lots of men getting semis at the sound of steam whistles. Myself included.

The usual argument about restoring locos has broken out. Locos are a touchy subject in the railway enthusiast's community.

They're all very excited because they think the station has been saved now.

I nod along.

My mum is here too. She told me Aunty Mandy won't be dropping by any time soon. I don't know where she went but she went away for a few weeks. She seems ok.

She's a bit lost in the evenings. Not sure what to do.

I tried to encourage her to join a book club.

(Mel) "When do I have time to read?"

Zumba class.

(Zumba) "I'm not flapping around like a beach whale in front of a load of ald biddies"

Wine tasting.

(Mel) "Go on then"

	But we decided that probably wasn't a good idea.
(Mel)	"Since when did you become so smart?"
	"Thanks for coming today mum"
(Mel)	"Come on, let's have a selfie."
	She's also joined Instagram. It mainly involves her liking pictures of babies and dogs and sometimes baby dogs. She's following me and wants to know why I haven't followed her back.
	Truth is, I haven't been on in a while.
	Someone taps me on the shoulder. I turn.
	Joey.
(Joey)	"Thought I'd find you here."
Nothing.	
(Joey)	"You're looking well."
Nothing.	
(Joey)	"Dom, can we go somewhere to talk?"
	I'd like to go back several weeks. But we can't.
(Joey)	"OK I'll tell you here. I wanted to let you know I'm moving back to Cheshire. I've been chatting to my ex. We're gonna give it another go. I wanted to talk to you before I left."

"Well you have."

(Joey) "Yeah I guess I have. I did have fun with you mate."

He turns and starts walking away.

For the first time in a long time Peter isn't watching me.

(Mel) "We going home?"

"Give me five minutes."

(Mel) "Chippy tea tonight."

It's just me now. Me at the station. No meets, no dates, just me.

I step out onto the platform and look down the tracks one more time.

It seems different.

Things have changed.

They're better now.

It wasn't my fault.

And I'm putting it all behind me.

That's what I have to do.

That's the right thing to do.

Because ultimately, I won.

Y'know.

I won.

There is a moment of silence.

Dom looks at the audience, considers what he has just said. Considers the truth of it.

He looks for reassurance. Or rejection.

He smiles.

Is he smiling?

The silence goes on a little longer than feels comfortable.

THE END